WHEN QUILT MAKING BECOMES WORSHIP

God's Love Hugs

Maxine and Geoff Brayshaw

A catalogue record for this book is available from the National Library of Australia

Copyright © 2021 Maxine and Geoff Brayshaw
All rights reserved.
ISBN-13: 978-1-922343-66-6

Linellen Press
265 Boomerang Road
Oldbury, Western Australia
www.linellenpress.com.au

Maxine blesses the hearts of many by gifting them with her beautifully sewn quilts and sharing the love of Christ.

Prophetic in nature, the quilts are given in such a way that it is clear the Holy Spirit has led Maxine in the giving.

Thanks, Maxine

xoxo, Jess

Having spent 15 of the most significant years of my life in Kenya, I received a quilt made for me by Maxine.

It meant so much to me, now so even more to have it with me in Australia. It tells a story of my time there, a lovely reminder…

Asante Sana,

Jody X

When I think of Maxine, sanctified imagination comes to mind …

Nikita

Contents

Contents v

About Maxine 1

Years of quilt making 3

Amazing God 4

Life of an evangelist 6

Turning seventy 7

Thanking carers 8

Comfort quilt 10

Swallows come 11

God knows every need 12

Lord's timing 13

A love hug 15

Inspired to give 16

Footsteps 18

Fruit of the Spirit 20

Psalm 23 21

African memories 23

South African roses 26

A tree of hope 27

A quilt that speaks 28

Being led	30
Through trials	31
God wraps presents	32
Blessing babies	34
The path and the door	35
Living stones	37
Living waters	38
God knows all things	39
Personalised gifts	41
Help from the Lord	42
Making old things new	43
Keep going	44
Replacement	45
Joyful and strong	50
A quiet achiever	51
Pouring out	52
Ask the Lord	54
True colours	56
God incident	57
A family's quilt	58
Passing on the baton	61
A quilt's story (by Maya)	63
Beyond quilt making (by Maya)	65

About Maxine

Over many years I have had fun creating something from 'nothing', using what God has provided. Materials just appeared to come my way, inspiring me with colours and patterns I would never have chosen, but which broadened my abilities and therefore the quilt patterns that emerged.

I want to use my time and energy to bless others. Giving a surprise to someone awesome. In this modern world of ours, it does not happen much.

God keeps blessing me to bless others to whom He wants to show His love.

The Bible mentions a lady who had blessed many people with her talent for sewing. Her name was Tabitha.

We are all given different talents. Just imagine the world receiving all the blessings that God has given us to give to others.

Wow!

Years of quilt making

For many years I made quilts like this for people, thinking it was my idea.

I never gave God the glory until He showed me in no uncertain way that He was using my hands for His work.

But it all changed when I went to America.

Amazing God

I was in America trying to be still and hear God's voice.

The last thing I anticipated was to have a dream to make a quilt for my sister-in-law. I knew it was for her, and I knew it was to have the apron in the middle and the background to be made of the material she had given me previously.

When I returned home, I learned she was celebrating her 60th birthday in a few weeks' time. Her daughter said she wanted no fuss.

The apron in the quilt had been given to me by my mother, and may well have come from her mother. I completed the embroidery and made the tennis racquet to signify tennis as it was a big part of her life. The book was sent to her daughter, who got the children to draw a picture. The hearts represent her three girls and one boy. And the teapot, cup and apron represent her gift of hospitality. The slate is part of her job as a teacher, but the lady on the quilt and the slate were not of my sister-in-law's time period.

As I was sewing, I was asking myself why I had

done it this way? The answer in my heart was that the quilt is about yesterday, today, and tomorrow.

It finally made sense and showed me that it is not me who is putting these quilts together. It is the Lord working through me.

What an amazing God we serve.

Since then, the quilt making has become a joyful adventure and mindful partnership with the Lord.

Life of an evangelist

The Lord showed me this quilt was to be in blue and white. The lady who received it loves blue and white China.

The top three squares represent love, joy, and peace.

The cross, her work as an evangelist.

The vase, her lovely aroma.

The candle is the light she sheds, and the cup with a saucer, her hospitality.

Turning seventy

I have been attending exercise classes for a number of years with a group of ladies who share problems associated with bone density. We have shared many a life story over the years.

I made a quilt for my exercise ladies as they turned seventy, each one totally different from the last but speaking to each person individually.

This quilt went to Helen, a lady from Malaysia of Chinese upbringing.

Thanking carers

The backing material often inspires the front.

This one went to a beautiful lady who has been a sleep shift worker in my brother's house.

My brother has brain damage and lives with four other men with disabilities.

Over the years many carers have received a quilt to thank them for their lovely work.

Comfort quilt

I was asked to help a lady by creating a quilt for her to match her painting. She was overcoming drug addiction.

She has since died from a brain tumour. I was told she was clutching her quilt at the end.

It was a privilege to be used to give her comfort.

Swallows come

Some of the quilts had words of encouragement.
The swallows came to Fionn in times of need.
The quilt backing had swallows as well.

My husband made suggestions to make Fionn's letters smaller and place the birds on the front to complete the picture. I have learnt to listen to his wisdom and suggestions with getting me to a better finish.

God knows every need

I found these beautifully worked cross-stitched dogs in the op shop where I find many blessings.

When I went looking for the backing material, I found one that matched the leaves on the front perfectly.

God knows our every need.

Lord's timing

I had been given some lovely swatches from a curtain shop, and this magnificent owl came forth.

I asked the Lord who it was for, and I knew it was for a young man called Mark, who was suffering a severe disability. His sister likewise has a major disability.

I picked up the quilt and left it at my friend's home.

When my friend called that night, she asked if I knew that it was their birthdays. One had been that day, and one was the following Wednesday.

I am always amazed at the Lord's timing.

A love hug

The brother received the owl quilt, and this is the sister's quilt.

She had trouble saying "rug" and called it a "love hug".

I thought her expression was very cute, so I continued to tell people that the Lord was giving them a love hug when they received a quilt.

Inspired to give

I attend a wonderful group each week for people overcoming drug and alcohol addictions.

In the drug world, it is a matter of "if I do or give you anything I expect to be compensated".

Often, I feel inspired to make a special gift for a person who has little self-esteem and no expectations.

Footsteps

A man I met at the group meetings was having trouble getting out of the front door of his house. He was too obese and unable to overcome his problems.

I made him the quilt with footsteps, and he loved his quilt.

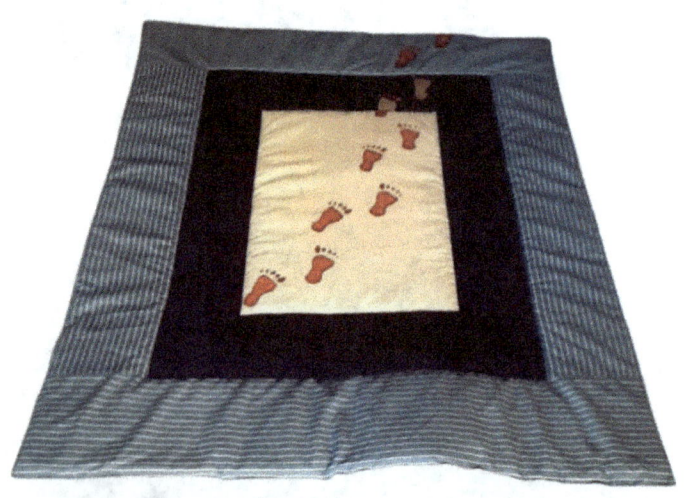

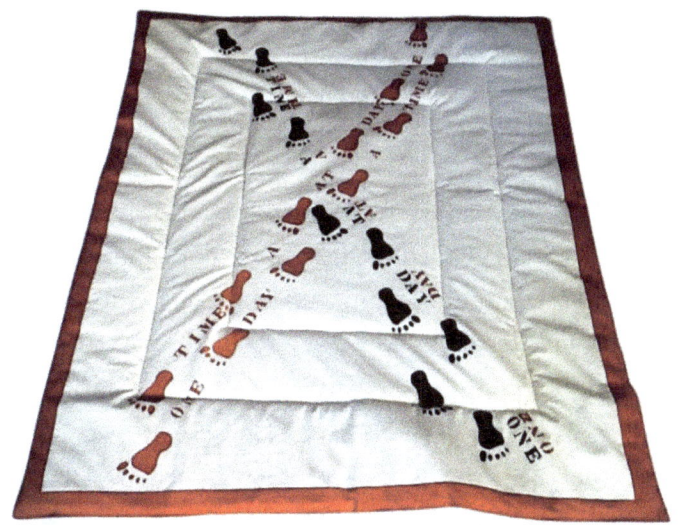

But a few years later, he went downhill. His unit, including the quilt, was taken over by someone else. He asked me for another quilt.

I usually have trouble obliging but have found God is much more generous than I. Before the meeting was finished, I knew the pattern of his new quilt.

Fruit of the Spirit

The new pattern was the fruit of the Spirit.
The man needed all the fruit to cope himself as he moved to another unit with someone who needed help with feeding and washing.

Psalm 23

I was making this hanging for the leader of the group meetings. It all fell into place after we had studied the twenty-third psalm.

> Psalm 23
>
> God is my Fierce Protector and my Provider.
> I always have more than enough.
> Like a Shepherd He finds a resting place for me
> In His luxury love.
> His Tracks take me to the quiet brooks of bliss,
> an oasis of grace.
> That's where He restores and revives my life.
> He opens before me pathways to God's pleasure.
> Leading me along in His footsteps of righteousness,
> So that I can bring honor to His name.
> Even when His path takes me through
> The valley of deepest darkness
> Fear will not conquer me, for You already have!
> Forever close to me, You will lead me through it all the way.
> The strength of Your authority is my peace, my reassurance.
> The comfort of Your love takes away my fear.
> I'll never be lonely when You are near.
> You become my delicious feast
> Even when my enemies dare to fight
> You anoint me with the fragrance of Your Holy Spirit,
> You give me all I can drink of You until my heart overflows.
> Why would I fear the future? For Your goodness and unfailing love,
> Will always be my companions every day;
> Then afterwards — when my life is through
> I'll return to Your glorious presence
> Forever with You!

I walked into my local op shop and found a nativity scene. The lamb was perfect.

When it was the day of presenting him with the hanging, he shared that he was prayed for, and he received the message to go towards the sun. He was so amazed when he looked at the picture.

God is good.

African memories

Many African quilts have come to life.
They bring back memories for people God has bought to this land.

The quilt below went back to Mozambique after the family had their fifth child. They are doing the Lord's work there.

South African roses

This quilt was given to a lovely lady from church. She told me later how she loved roses and missed the roses she had grown in South Africa.

It was like God blessing her and providing her with good memories.

Mauve was her favourite colour too.

A tree of hope

A friend's friend named Wendy had been diagnosed with cancer. She was coming up to Perth from Mandurah on the Monday for a doctor's visit.

My friend asked me to make Wendy a quilt. I told her I had already started working on a quilt with a big tree in the middle. My friend said that was appropriate as Wendy had bought a unit because she fell in love with the tree in front of the unit.

The quilt was finished in time for her visit. The diagnosis was not a good one, and the word 'hope' was timely.

A quilt that speaks

Several weeks later, I asked my friend how Wendy was fairing. She said she was doing O.K.

But Wendy's nieces from two families were in Princess Margaret Hospital with leukemia. The first little girl's treatment left her blind.

The decals on the quilt could be used as a Braille quilt.

I didn't know of the girl's blindness until later, but our God knows all things.

The other girl, Charlotte, received the quilt below.

Being led

I was led to take this quilt for a man at our recovery meeting. I did not know why nor that he was picking up a little girl from school that day.

There was an altercation with a drug-affected person. Police were called, and the little girl was traumatised.

The little girl fell asleep covered with her 'love hug' in the car going home.

Through trials

My girlfriend's sister had just been diagnosed with breast cancer. I had just attended a quilt fair and come across this beautiful panel.

There have been many more quilts for people going through trials such as breast cancer. Breast cancer is something I can relate to, having been through it myself.

Our God knows what will bring comfort to others.

God wraps presents

I met a lovely young pre-school teacher at church one day.

She was telling me about a boy at her work who has autism. She said he slept for three hours a day and did not talk much. His first word was 'elephant', and his name was Jack. She asked me if I could make a quilt for Jack.

I love a challenge, and the quilt was made that week.

When she saw it, she told me she had bought paper to wrap it that was coloured with the same two blues as on the quilt.

What an exciting life we live following where God leads.

Blessing babies

This quilt was already finished, so I placed it in the car and headed off to church. Once there, I found it was to be an infant dedication. Another lady was painting a beautiful picture of mother and baby in Jesus' hands. I felt the urge to offer my quilt.

The baby was dressed in mauve, which was the mother's favourite colour. She was thrilled to see her baby blessed.

The butterflies also meant a lot to her.

The path and the door

I was once asked by one of the men from the drug rehabilitation group to make a quilt for his grandson. He said he needed protection from the atmosphere he was being brought up in. This quilt design is what eventually came to me.

Revelation 3:20: "Behold, I stand at the door and knock; if anyone hears My voice and opens the door, I will come in to him and will dine with him, and he with Me." (NASB)

John14:6: "I am the way, and the truth, and the life; no one comes to the Father except through Me." (NASB)

The path showing the way to the door has significant meaning in the context of this quilt.

The mother hen protecting her chicks along the path also spoke to me.

Living stones

This quilt is a powerful representation of living stones and a strong foundation.

The window also meant something to the receiver as he had just had a dream about a window.

Living waters

Psalm 1 speaks to a person overcoming drug addictions: the tree roots going deep into living water, yielding fruit in season, and not going back to the old ways of walking with the wicked.

God knows all things

This was a remarkable story where I made a quilt for my girlfriend's mother.

My friend thought it was about her childhood when her mother made potions as a chemist.

When her mother received the quilt, she was reminded of a gift her daughter had bought her in China: identical bottles to the ones on the quilt.

God knows all things.

Personalised gifts

A friend asked me to make a quilt for her friend.

This beautiful cross-stitch was another find at an op shop. I was able to work her name into the piece to make it personalised.

The friend was a marine biologist.

How amazing is our God!

Help from the Lord

This one went to a granddaughter of one of the ladies I attend exercises with.

The lady was very concerned for her granddaughter as she was suffering from an eating disorder.

Psalm 121: 1-2: "I lift up my eyes to the mountains—where does my help come from? My help comes from the Lord, the Maker of heaven and earth." (NIV)

Making old things new

This quilt reminds me of how God can make old things new again.

The doilies, the background material, and the strips in between were all donations.

What we think is obsolete, God can still bless someone with as if a new creation. Wow!

Keep going

This rather weird creation went to our exercise leader who was having his first child, a little girl.

This was given on behalf of his class of seventy and eighty-year-old women that he pushes to keep going. He was thrilled and keeps us informed of his baby's developments.

Replacement

I made this quilt at the beginning of the year and was proud of the finished product.

It went to a new grandson of my friend from the group meetings. I had previously made three other quilts for this boy's siblings.

Unfortunately, the family went through a terrible time of trauma and ended up in a women's refuge with all their 'love hugs' and their clothes burnt and thrown out.

Their grandfather came to me and asked me for a favour to replace the quilts as the children had trouble sleeping.

One week later, four quilts were completed, and a spare one went to the mother.

Grace is three and would have grown up with the previous quilt I had made for her sister in 2016. The one that comforts her now has a similar pattern.

Big sister, Lilly, is eleven, so she received a more mature quilt.

The baby's quilt had an alphabet panel which is nothing like his previous Noah one.

I really regretted the destruction these children had witnessed. I know God can bind up the brokenhearted.

The 7-year-old boy's quilt was slightly different from his first one but still had wildlife on it.

He previously received a frog quilt, so this was similar, but different.

Joyful and strong

God has given me a heart for the young people in our church.

This quilt is joyful and strong like the young lady who received it.

A quiet achiever

This went to a beautiful quiet achiever.

Her husband commented on how the colours match in with their home. I have never been to their home.

Pouring out

Frogs come in handy to whip up a quick quilt.

My stencils get lots of use, and I thank God for His provision in materials. People donate to me their castoffs, and God puts them to use.

It is like the widow who poured out the oil into jars (2 Kings 4). My material supply does not run out.

Ask the Lord

I gave this quilt to a young lady at church who was going through a period of turmoil.

She then responded by turning around and asking me what the colours meant. She was a little worried that the black was God pointing out her sins.

I was dumbfounded as I had not asked the Lord. So, I asked, and He answered.

The black was God's power and strength, and with two borders of black, she had a double portion surrounding her.

Purple, His royalty.
Pink, His loving heart.
Yellow, His joy for her.
Orange, His fire and warmth.
White, His cleansing.

My problem was I forgot to ask.

True colours

God has given me an eye for colour. It inspires me and gets me started.

I have no idea how any of the quilts I have made will be received but, time after time, the recipient mentions the colour is perfect for the room or their life.

God knows all!

God incident

I made some quilts for a group of mothers from our church.

I hadn't met the mothers but made this for one little boy. The mother who received it sent me this photo.

I thought she must have gone home and dressed her baby to match the quilt, but I was told this was the outfit he was wearing when he received it.

I was blown away with this 'God incident'.

A family's quilt

Seventeen years ago, I was asked to make a quilt for my sister-in-law's mother, Mrs Paganoni. Mrs Pag was turning seventy-five.

Coming from Italy, we placed the red, white and green around the edges.

The trunk of the tree was the basis for this family treasure. The different family members initially placed their handprints, and subsequent grandchildren have had their footprints inserted. Some family members are now gone but not forgotten.

There is even a dog print of her favourite companion.

The back was signed by her family and represented Mrs Pag's life: a great cook, the family farm, bowling and cards. The seed packets stand for her love of gardening.

Mrs Pag is now ninety-two and her quilt means a lot to her.

Passing on the baton

Earlier this year, my granddaughter Grace did some stenciling with me, so we decided to carry on and sew her pieces together.

It took much time and effort as the COVID lockdown stopped us from meeting, and she was unable to get the materials in the country town where she lived.

I was amazed that, months later, Grace had her finished product.

I remember my gran showing me how to use her treadle sewing machine and many, many hours of enjoyment have been the result. I pray Grace continues with her talent and maybe one day passes it on to another generation.

A quilt's story (by Maya)

The quilt Maxine made for me is a true representation of my life.

The backing material is purple and black, which represents my old life of seeking.

I knew God existed, but I did not know Him personally. My journey was highly spiritual (represented by purple) but always painful (black).

But then, the Lord bought my past by his blood (red trimming), birthed me anew (green), deposited His Spirit in me (purple) and brought me into His presence and ongoing communion with Him (blue).

The two flowers at the centre is an ongoing theme of my life. Old mindsets, unhealthy habits of thought and behaviours, are dying off (dying flower) and continually being replaced by new ways—Lord's ways (living flowers).

The Holy Spirit helps me see what of my past needs to wither and die, and He grants me grace to let go and receive the Lord's ways.

Every day something dies in the 'tomb' of Jesus Christ and gets born in the 'womb' of the Father.

Every day I am looking more and more like the person my Father created me to be—free, joyful, and loving.

2 Corinthians 3:18: 'And we all, with unveiled face, continually seeing as in a mirror the glory of the Lord, are progressively being transformed into His image from [one degree of] glory to [even more] glory, which comes from the Lord, [who is] the Spirit.' (AMP)

Beyond quilt making (by Maya)

Such a profound image we see and recognise in Maxine, of God inspiring our thoughts, taking us beyond our understanding, and providing all the resources we need.

Maxine's refuge is at the foot of Jesus Christ with her spirit, mind, emotions, will and body completely surrendered to Him.

There is such an alignment and communion with the Lord that Maxine and the Lord become one. These are the moments when Maxine is questioning, "Is it me, or the Lord working through me?"

Maxine holds nothing back but gives it all to the Lord, so He can move through her and speak His words through her hands.

The Lord feeds Maxine's mind with ideas, floods her emotions with joy and peace, and her hand starts sewing quilts that speak—quilts that continue to speak.

Maxine's quilts speak the Father's love, redemption, healing, and deliverance.

Psalm 68:11: 'The Lord gives the word [of power]; the women who bear and publish [the news] are a great host.' (AMPC)

The Holy Father is so delighted with Maxine, as the two of them work together to bless Maxine's brothers and sisters and His other children.

Maxine's 'passing on the baton' goes beyond teaching others, like her granddaughter Grace, to sew.

She has taught me how to work with the Lord.

Maxine has taught me a lifestyle of worship.

www.ingramcontent.com/pod-product-compliance
Lightning Source LLC
Chambersburg PA
CBHW071541080526
44588CB00011B/1740